HOW TO STOP BEING TOXIC

A guide to stop hurting people you love,Build Empathy, Heal Your Mind, Unlearn Toxic Thoughts, Emotions and Behaviors

Copyright

Except in the case of a brief citation embodied in critical reviews and certain other commercial uses permitted by brand law, no part of this publication may be reproduced, distributed, or transmitted in any form or by any means, including photocopying, recording, or other electronic or mechanical styles, without the publisher's prior written authorization.

ABOUT THE AUTHOR

Lucky Willis, a devoted family man and seasoned author in the realm of personal transformation and self-help, is a name synonymous with inspiration and growth. Married with three children, His life experiences have woven a rich tapestry of wisdom and insight that he shares with his readers.

Lucky Willis journey into the world of personal development began with his own quest for self-improvement. Armed with determination and a thirst for knowledge, he delved into various fields of study, gathering insights and techniques that would later form the foundation of his writing. His academic pursuits provided him with a solid understanding of human psychology, motivation, and behavior.

With his inherent gift for writing and a deep empathy for the human condition, He embarked on a mission to empower others to unlock their full potential. Drawing from his own life lessons, as well as from the experiences of those around him, he crafts compelling narratives that resonate with readers on a personal level.In a world filled with self-help gurus and motivational speakers, Lucky Willis stands out for his sincerity and depth. His writing transcends the superficial, offering readers a transformative journey towards self-discovery and fulfillment. As long as there are individuals seeking growth and meaning in their lives, His words will continue to serve as beacons of hope and guidance.

Table of content

Conclusion: Recap: Key Takeaways and Continued Growth

Introduction

Hi there, and welcome to the adventure. "How to Stop Being Toxic" is a guide for introspection and personal growth. You will travel through these pages to: Recognize the causes of toxicity and the effects it has on you and those around you. Investigate the root origins of your harmful inclinations. Cultivate self-compassion as a solid foundation for transformation. Develop good communication skills and empathy to build greater bonds with others. Discover useful methods and strategies for stress management, dispelling unfavorable ideas, and fostering resilience. Learn the value of healthy behaviors and self-care for your general well-being. To move past old hurts, navigate forgiveness and conflict resolution. Accept the influence of having a strong support network to envelop oneself in positive energy. This book is not about blaming or making fun of you for past transgressions. It's about giving you the confidence to own your development and create a happier, healthier life. Remember that it takes time and work to bring about change as you set out on this path of self-discovery. Never stop learning and developing; instead, enjoy your accomplishments and have patience with yourself. Now let's get started!

Chapter 1: What is Toxicity and How Does it Affect You and Others?

This chapter delves into the idea of relationship toxicity, examining how it might impair your relationships and general wellbeing. We'll define toxic behaviors, explain how they affect people around you, and give you the skills you need to spot toxic behaviors in yourself.

Defined toxic Conduct Recognizing Unhealthy Patterns

This section goes deep into the fundamental traits of harmful actions. It examines the distinctions between constructive conflicts and destructive tendencies of negativity, manipulation, or control.

Prioritize Results Over Process: In order to achieve mutual understanding, healthy conflicts require open communication of opposing points of view. Regardless of the merits of the problem, toxic actions frequently place a higher priority on winning debates or demeaning the other person.

Power imbalances: In order to be healthy, relationships must be reciprocal. One-sided communication dynamics, in which one person dominates or ignores the needs and feelings of the other, can give rise to toxic behaviors. Unhealthy Communication Approaches: Relationship-damaging toxic communication patterns include name-calling, yelling, silent treatment, and persistent criticism.

 Common Instances of Hazardous Behaviors: We'll use a variety of examples to show harmful practices in various communication modalities. This could consist of: Chronic Negativity: If you have a constantly pessimistic attitude, people around you may also feel that way. This can include dwelling on the worst-case scenario, moaning all the time, or discounting good events. Shifting the Blame: A vital component of wholesome relationships is accepting accountability for your deeds. Shifting the blame elsewhere entails accepting responsibility for the problem even though you were part of it.

Excessive Criticism: While constructive criticism has its advantages, it can turn toxic when it becomes overly harsh or concentrates on disparaging specific people. Unhealthy jealousy and possessiveness can be oppressive and impede a partner's ability to express their individuality and independence. Emotional manipulation is the practice of utilizing feelings of guilt, force, or control over the actions of another person. Threats, playing the victim, and silent treatments are just a few of the various ways it manifests.

The Spectrum of Toxicity: It's critical to recognize that there is a spectrum of toxicity. The distinction between sporadic outbursts and ingrained destructive behavior patterns is covered in this subchapter.

Isolated Events: Errors happen to everyone. It's not always a sign of toxicity to say something nasty in a heated situation every now and then. What counts is owning up to the error, expressing regret, and making an effort to improve. Habitual Patterns: Toxic habits indicate a deeper problem that needs to be addressed when they start to occur frequently in your interactions. Tools to recognize and deal with these patterns are included in this chapter.

How Toxicity Affects Relationships
Erosion of Trust

The basis of wholesome relationships is trust, and this subchapter examines how toxic actions can undermine it. We'll talk about how a breach of trust can cause worry, insecurity, and trouble establishing positive relationships.

Broken Promises & Dishonesty: It is difficult to feel safe and secure in a relationship when someone constantly betrays trust or tells falsehoods.

Unpredictable Behavior: Unpredictable behavior from toxic people can make people nervous and cautious. Negative Emotional Impact: You may feel emotionally depleted and ignored after engaging in toxic encounters. The effect of negativity and manipulation on your emotional health is examined in this subchapter. Emotional weariness: Being with people who continually sap your vitality with their negativity can be emotionally taxing.

Invalidation of Feelings: You may feel invisible and inconsequential if your experiences and feelings are downplayed or ignored.

Negative Cycle Dynamics: We'll examine the ways in which toxic behaviors can set off unfavorable patterns in relationships. This could entail defensive and accusatory behavior patterns or difficulties communicating effectively.

Attack Patterns and Blame Games: When couples engage in these behaviors, neither one accepts accountability for their actions, and issues go unsolved.

Stonewalling and Communication Breakdown: Isolating oneself or refusing to talk during arguments causes a rift and obstructs amicable solutions.

Identifying Your Own Indices of Toxicity Techniques for Self-Assessment

You can use the exercises and suggestions in this section to discover any potential hazardous places in yourself. One of these exercises could be keeping a journal.

Thinking Back on Previous Conflicts: Go over previous disputes or arguments. Did you prioritize winning the argument over comprehending the other person's point of view? Have you taken any Thinking Back on Previous Conflicts: Go over previous disputes or arguments. Did you prioritize winning the argument over comprehending the other person's point of view? Did you own up to your part in the matter, or did you place the blame elsewhere? How did the other person and you feel

about the conflict? Think About the Impact of Your Actions on Others: Consider the usual effects of your words and deeds on the people you love. Do they experience love and support, or do they experience criticism, silence, or emotional exhaustion?
Owning Your Mistakes: Acknowledging your part in toxic dynamics is essential to identifying toxicity. This chapter stresses the significance of accepting accountability for your deeds without descending into self-blame.
Acknowledging Accountability: Owning up to your mistakes does not entail self-punishment. It entails owning up to your errors and being prepared to grow from them.
The Power of Apologies: Broken relationships can be greatly restored with a heartfelt apology. When offering an apology, emphasize that you are sorry for what you did and that you will try to do better.
Seeking Honest Feedback: We'll talk about how important it is to ask family members or close friends for their honest opinions. This can give you important information about how other people could interpret your actions.
Selecting the Correct People: Seek for those who will be forthright with you while also being sincere and encouraging.
Openness to Feedback: Take constructive criticism to heart and see it as a chance to improve.

Recall that acknowledging your own toxicity is the first step toward making a change for the better. Although facing your flaws can be painful, doing so is an essential first step in creating stronger bonds with other people.

How to stop being toxic by Lucky Willis

You will gain skills and techniques in the upcoming chapters to develop emotional health, effective communication, and empathy. You and others around you will ultimately live more fulfilled lives as a result of this empowering self-discovery adventure.

Chapter 2: Exploring the Roots of Toxicity

Making a positive change in your behavior requires first understanding its source. This chapter explores the possible root causes of toxicity and how your interactions with others can be impacted by past experiences, thought habits, and emotional triggers.

The Impact of Prior Experiences

Our identity is shaped by our prior experiences, and bad experiences might occasionally have a long-lasting effect on our actions. This chapter looks at the role that the past plays in creating harmful attitudes. Childhood Trauma: Being abused emotionally, physically, or sexually as a child can cause problems as an adult in terms of intimacy, trust, and communication. Recognizing that you are not alone if you suffered trauma as a youngster is crucial. Therapy is frequently effective for helping people process their prior experiences and create healthy coping strategies. Models of unhealthy relationships: You may normalize or even take on toxic behaviors in your own interactions if you were raised in or around toxic relationships. You might find problematic patterns you may be unknowingly repeating by thinking back on the dynamics you saw in your family or close relationships.
Types of Attachments: The study of attachment theory looks at how our early interactions with our caregivers

influence our social interactions as adults. Relationship challenges including trust and emotional intimacy can be attributed to insecure attachment patterns, such as anxious or avoidant attachment. You may learn more about your attachment style and create better attachment patterns with the aid of accessible resources.

Unhealthy Patterns of Thought

Our emotions and actions are greatly influenced by our thinking. This chapter examines the ways in which poisonous inclinations can be fueled by faulty or negative thought processes. Cognitive distortions are automatic, unfavorable cognitive habits that might cause people to misread events and increase their emotional sensitivity. Typical cognitive distortions include: excessive perception of objects (all-or-nothing thinking) Overgeneralization refers to drawing strong unfavorable inferences from one or two incidents. Reading people's minds (assumptions, without proof, what they are thinking) Emotional reasoning: the conviction that your feelings are true Low Self-Esteem: Being insecure or harboring a bad opinion of oneself can make one defensive, envious, or control-obsessed in relationships. Emphasizing your strengths, engaging in self-compassion exercises, and establishing reasonable goals for yourself are all part of developing self-esteem. Fear of Abandonment: An intense dread of being abandoned can show up in relationships as clinging, possessiveness, or dominating tendencies.

Relationships that are more safe and trustworthy can be developed by investigating the source of this fear and creating effective coping techniques.

Triggers and Reactions on an Emotional Level

Everybody has emotional triggers, which are events or actions that cause intense emotional reactions. This section looks at how you can prevent toxic reactions by being aware of your triggers and developing healthy coping skills.

Finding Your Triggers: Take note of circumstances or actions that frequently cause you to experience intensely negative feelings. You can learn to recognize your triggers by keeping a journal or consulting a therapist.

Knowing Your Emotional Reaction: After determining what your triggers are, investigate the feelings they make you feel. Are you experiencing fear, hurt, or anger? Being aware of the underlying feelings can enable you to react in a more positive way.

Creating Healthy Coping Mechanisms: Create healthy coping mechanisms in place of impulsive reactions to triggers. These could be mindfulness exercises, deep breathing exercises, or stepping away from the situation for a moment to collect oneself before reacting.

Expressing Your Needs: At times, being honest and forthright with someone else about what you need might help you avoid being triggered. Tell them what sets you off and how they can help you the most when that happens. Recall that identifying the causes of toxicity is a continuous effort. Celebrate your accomplishments and have patience with yourself. The upcoming chapters will provide you with the knowledge and techniques you need to control your emotions, increase empathy, and improve your communication abilities—all essential elements in creating a happy and satisfying relationship.

Chapter 3: The Importance of Self-Compassion

Healthy connections with others and with yourself start with developing self-compassion. It gives you the ability to face your flaws and difficulties with compassion and empathy, which builds resilience and inner strength. This chapter examines techniques for developing self-compassion as well as the significance of it.

Overcoming Self-Critic Thoughts

That voice in our heads that highlights our weaknesses and flaws is our inner critic. Although a healthy dose of self-criticism can spur us on to greater success, an extreme inner critic can be extremely detrimental to our well being and sense of self. How to recognize and confront these negative self-talk tendencies is covered in this subchapter. How to Spot Your Inner Critic Be mindful of the internal dialogue you have with yourself. When you feel nervous or make a mistake, what thoughts do you tell yourself? Recognizing the Effects: Think about how the voice of your inner critic makes you feel. Does it make you feel guilty, nervous, or like you want to avoid people? Challenging Negative Thoughts: After you've recognized negative patterns of self-talk, take steps to refute them. Are these ideas warped by your inner critic, or are they grounded in reality? Consider asking yourself, "Would I talk to a friend this way?" Alternatively "Is there evidence to support this thought?"

Creating a Voice of Compassion: Use a caring voice to silence your inner critic. What would a friend who is encouraging say to you if they were to speak with you? Practice being gentle and understanding with yourself.

Putting Self-Acceptance Into Practice

Self-acceptance is accepting your shortcomings and inadequacies without passing judgment on them. Realizing your worth as a person despite your flaws and vulnerabilities is crucial. The techniques for developing self-acceptance are examined in this subchapter.

Embracing Your Humanity: Everyone has difficulties and makes mistakes. Acknowledging that your flaws are not unique to you can be a significant step in the direction of self-acceptance. Exercises in mindfulness can help you become more conscious of your thoughts and feelings without passing judgment. This enables you to acknowledge your inner critic without succumbing to its pessimism. Self-acceptance can be aided by methods such as attentive breathing or meditation.

Gratitude exercises: You can develop a positive outlook and a sense of value by concentrating on the aspects of your life, yourself, and the people in it. Write down a few things you are grateful for every day or keep a gratitude diary.

Letting Go of Perfectionism: Aiming for perfection is a harmful and unachievable objective. Celebrate all of your accomplishments, no matter how modest, and instead concentrate on your growth.

Developing Self-Respect

Your total feeling of worth and value in yourself is called self-esteem. This chapter looks at developing healthy self-esteem independent of outside approval. Identifying Your Strengths: Enumerate your assets, skills, and commendable traits. Think back on your prior achievements and acquired abilities. Acknowledging your advantages can increase your self-assurance and self-worth.
Establishing Achievable Goals: A sense of accomplishment and self-worth can be enhanced by setting reasonable goals and acknowledging your work toward them.
Healthy Self-Care: Developing self-esteem requires attending to your mental and physical well-being. This entails obtaining adequate rest, consuming wholesome foods, and taking part in enjoyable activities.
Creating Healthy Relationships: Having a positive, encouraging circle of people who accept you for who you are can have a big impact on your self-esteem.

Recall that developing healthy self-esteem and self-compassion is a journey, not a destination. There will be obstacles on your path, but you may cultivate a more loving and accepting relationship with yourself through persistent practice and effort. Building on this foundation, the upcoming chapters will examine techniques for developing empathy, communicating clearly, and fostering positive relationships.

Chapter 4: The Power of Empathy

Knowing and being able to share another person's emotions is empathy. It's essential to having wholesome interactions and enables you to have stronger connections with people. The value of empathy is examined in this chapter along with strategies for developing it in your relationships.

Appreciating Many Viewpoints

People experience life differently because the world is a varied place. This chapter delves into the value of developing empathy by considering things from another person's point of view.

Experience as a Lens: Our life experiences mold our perspective on the world. Think of the ways that your own experiences and background shape your ideas and emotions.

preconceptions to appreciation:All of us harbor preconceptions, unconscious ideas, or biases. Knowing your prejudices can enable you to avoid misinterpreting events or passing unjust judgments on other people.

Exercises in Taking Perspective: Get comfortable placing yourself in other people's shoes. Think about a circumstance from their point of view and what emotions they might be experiencing. Practice taking perspectives using role-playing or writing task.

Building emotional intelligence

 Understanding, using, and positively managing your own emotions is known as emotional intelligence, or EQ. Comprehension of other people's emotions is another aspect of it. This subchapter looks at how raising your EQ can improve your empathy.

Recognizing Your Emotions: Recognizing your emotions is the first step toward controlling them. Listen to your thoughts and physical feelings to determine how you're feeling in various circumstances.

Emotional Regulation: You can acquire good techniques to control your emotions once you recognize them. Writing, journaling, or speaking with a reliable friend could all be part of this.

Empathy and Emotional Intelligence: You are better able to perceive and react to the emotions of others when you are conscious of and competent in controlling your own emotions.

 The Active Listening Skills: Active Listening is important than just hearing someone speak. It's about being attentive, getting the underlying meaning, and showing that you care. This subchapter looks at ways to listen actively that will increase empathy. Give It Your Whole Concentration Distractions should be put aside and the speaker should be your main attention. Maintain eye contact and don't cut others off. Verbal and Nonverbal Cues: Notice the speaker's words as well as their body language and voice tone. To be sure you comprehend, periodically summarize what you've heard. This shows the speaker you're paying attention and invites them to go into further detail. Pose Open-Ended Questions with several answers invite the speaker to go into further detail about their thoughts and experiences. Steer clear of yes or no questions that end a discussion. Responding with empathy is acknowledging the speaker's feelings and demonstrating that you get their viewpoint. You might comment, for instance, "I can see why you're upset" or "It sounds like you're feeling frustrated." Recall that developing empathy is a practiced and time-consuming ability. Honor your development and have patience with yourself. The chapters that come after will go into how to use empathy to develop constructive communication and handle disagreement in your relationships. Empathy will help you to build closer relationships and to make the world a happier and more accepting place for yourself and everyone around you. More Advice on Developing Empathy Read Fiction: You may get inside the heads of many individuals and comprehend their experiences by reading fiction. Practice Random Acts of Kindness: Showing kindness to others will increase your empathy and sense of connectedness to them. Volunteer: Giving of your time to an issue you support might open your eyes to many viewpoints and life experiences. These pointers can help you to keep improving your empathy and forge deeper relationships with those around you.

Chapter 5: Effective Communication for Healthy Relationships

The foundation of satisfying partnerships is communication. It helps us to connect and comprehend people by enabling us to express our needs, thoughts, and feelings with them. Misunderstandings, animosity, and conflict may all result from poor communication, regrettably. With the knowledge in this chapter, you can develop relationships that are stronger and healthier.

"I" Statement Art

"I" statements are a potent instrument for aggressive, non-blaming expression of your demands and feelings. They support your ability to own your feelings and steer clear of accusing words that can make people defensive. Basic "I" statement structure is as follows: "I feel [emotion] when [situation] because [need/want]." Benefits of Statements Beginning with "I" As you use "I" statements, you: Own your emotions. Make your needs plain. Inspire a more fruitful discussion. Statements Beginning with "I" Examples As opposed to "You never listen to me!" Try saying, "I feel like I'm not being heard when we talk. If you could alternately listen intently, it would be very appreciated." Instead of saying, "You're always so messy!" Try saying, "I need a spotless place to unwind, so I get overwhelmed when the living room is messy. Might we collaborate to set up a cleaning schedule?" The Nonviolent Communication Techniques Subchapter Marshall B. Rosenberg created the nonviolent communication (NVC) paradigm to encourage compassion and understanding in our relationships.

Four main elements are stressed by NVC: Observation: Present the circumstances impartially and without any bias. Identify your feelings in the circumstance. Needs: State the unfulfilled fundamental needs. Requests: Positively express a particular request of the other person. NVC can be used in a variety of communication situations, from handling more serious disputes to communicating small irritations. NVC benefits include the ability to: Become a better sympathetic listener. Declare your needs clearly and without blaming others. Encourage resolving conflicts more cooperatively. Case Studies of NVC "I notice there are still dishes to be done (observation). I need a clean kitchen to feel relaxed, so I'm feeling overwhelmed. After supper tonight, would you be willing to clean up? Request made.

Creating Healthy Boundaries

Personal rules called boundaries enable you to keep up good relationships. In your contacts with other people, they lay down what is and is not appropriate behavior. Boundaries are important because they allow for: Stewarding your mental and physical health. promoting in partnerships mutual respect. Staying away

How to stop being toxic by Lucky Willis

from burnout or resentment. Boundaries might be of the physical, emotional, mental, or material kinds. Establishing limits: Establishing limits is telling people exactly what you need and want. Among these could be: Deciding on requests that take up too much of your time or energy. Saying you need your own place. Clarifying the expectations for the frequency of communication. Putting Limits in Place Boundaries is only the beginning. When someone breaks your rules, it's just as crucial to stick to them. This can be expressing your needs again coolly but strongly or concluding a conversation with grace. Boundary-setting Examples "I appreciate you inviting me out, but tonight I'm feeling exhausted. Another time, I would really like to catch up." (Determining a social engagement limit) "I need to spend some time alone in the evenings. Could we decide when all of us have quiet time? (Creating a line separating emotional space) Recall that mastering good communication is a lifelong practice. With the help of these techniques and self-compassion, you can cultivate closer, more robust bonds with the people who really count. Chapters that follow will address forgiveness, dispute resolution, and preserving positive relationships—all of which are essential for negotiating the complexity of human connection.

Chapter 6: Conflict Resolution and Forgiveness: Building Stronger Bonds

Every partnership is going to have conflict. Unmet needs, different viewpoints, or just poor communication can all lead to disagreements and misunderstandings. This chapter gives you the skills you need to handle disagreement in a positive way and practice forgiveness, for yourself and for others, in order to create relationships that are more robust and durable.

Good Resolutions of Conflicts

Conflict doesn't have to be harmful. When you approach conflicts with a positive attitude and good communication techniques, you can make them into chances for development and comprehension. Put the Problem-Solving, Not the Blame, First: Turn away from blaming and toward cooperatively developing answers that meet the requirements of all parties. To really grasp the viewpoint of the other person, practice active listening techniques (discussed in Chapter 4). Use "I" statements (discussed in Chapter 5) to assertively and without accusation express your wants and feelings. Kind Communication: Throughout the argument, keep up a kind communication. Steer clear of interrupting, naming, and making personal remarks. Breaks: If feelings are running strong, pause the discussion to let them settle before carrying on. Communicating more effectively can result from returning to the problem with a more composed mind.

The Strength of Forgiveness (For Yourself and Others)

Emotionally taxing and impeding progress is holding onto anger and resentment. Giving up bad feelings and deciding to move forward is the process of forgiveness. It's releasing oneself from the weight of negativity, not necessarily endorsing the other person's behavior. Advantages of Forgiveness: Let forgiveness to: Simplify your life and feel better emotionally. Promove better connections. Help you to put the past behind you. Forgiveness is a Path,
Not a Place to Be: Forgiveness is a time- and effort-consuming individual process. It might not happen overnight, and there is no right or wrong way to forgive. Show yourself some patience. The hardest person to forgive is sometimes oneself. Give yourself permission to make mistakes in the past and concentrate on improving from them.
Setting Limits: Forgiveness does not include forgetting or putting oneself in a vulnerable situation once more. You can set appropriate limits to safeguard yourself going forward and yet forgive someone (discussed in Chapter 5).

Accompanying Conflict and Building trust

Accompanying Conflict Building trust and fortifying the relationship are as important to conflict resolution as settling the dispute. After a fight, take action to fix any harm that was done. This may be saying sorry sincerely, doing goodwill gestures, or just expressing your sympathy.

Developing Communication: Take use of the encounter to raise your level of communication. Talk about what went wrong and how you could communicate more successfully going forward. Rebuilding trust requires time and constant work. Reliability and honesty should be your top priorities, as should showing that you appreciate the partnership.

Letting Go and Getting On: Relationships can occasionally not be fixed, even with your best efforts. Those situations call for taking lessons from the past and proceeding gracefully. Recall that negotiating the complexity of human relationships requires the ability to resolve conflicts and forgive. With the people who count most, you may create stronger, more enduring relationships by using these strategies. The need of taking care of yourself and creating a supportive network will be discussed in the next chapter. These are two essential components of sustaining good relationships all of your life.

Chapter 7: Cognitive Behavioral Therapy (CBT) Techniques for Healthy Relationships

One type of psychotherapy that emphasizes the relationship between thoughts, feelings, and actions is called cognitive behavioral therapy, or CBT. It gives you the skills you need to recognize and resist unhelpful thought patterns that fuel poor behavior and emotional anguish. Core CBT strategies for creating and preserving healthy relationships are covered in this chapter.

Recognizing and Overcoming Negative Thought Patterns

We feel and act in our relationships largely because of the thoughts we have. This section goes into how to recognize and combat bad thought patterns that might ruin your relationships with other people. Automatic Negative Thoughts (ANTs) are twisted or useless ideas that enter your mind without warning under specific circumstances. Negative feelings and bad habits are frequently the results of them. In relationships, typical ANTs: Mind reading is assuming, without proof, that you know what the other person is thinking (e.g., "They're mad at me"). Fortune telling is predicting unjustified bad things to happen (e.g., "This friendship is doomed"). The act of exaggerating small issues (e.g., "If I say the wrong thing, they'll never want to talk to me again"). None at all thinking: extremes (e.g., "They're either my best friend or they hate me"). Overgeneralization is drawing general unfavorable inferences from one or two incidents (e.g., "Everyone always lets me down").

Finding Your ANTs Particularly when you experience bad feelings in your relationships, be aware of what you are thinking. Telling yourself what types of things about the other person or the situation? Fighting Your ANTs: Don't believe your ANTs when you've identified them. Inquire of oneself things like: "Is my fear talking, or is this thought supported by facts?" What is the situation's worst, best, and most likely result? "If a friend were thinking this way, what would I say to them?" Replacing Ants with More Realistic Concepts Reframe your unfavorable ideas and substitute more reasonable and fair ones.

Creating Well-Informed Coping Strategies

Relationship might suffer from unhealthy coping methods like anger or avoidance. This subchapter looks at how to build positive coping skills to handle challenging feelings in your relationships with other people. Recognizing Your Adaptive Strategies Think of

your usual relationship handling of difficult emotions. Are you withdrawn, hostile, or self-destructive?
Sustaining Adaptations: Deep breathing, meditation, and progressive muscle relaxation are some relaxation techniques that can help you to decompress right now. Journaling: Putting your ideas and emotions down in writing might help you to understand yourself and get perspective. Exercises in mindfulness can increase your awareness of, and ability to judge, your thoughts and feelings. Assertive communication is expressing your wants and feelings clearly and confidently while honoring the rights of the other person (discussed in Chapter 5).
Getting Help: Speaking with a therapist, counselor, or reliable friend can offer insightful advice and support.
Developing Your Toolbox of Coping Strategies: Investigate several healthy coping strategies and see which suits you the best. It is the aim to be equipped with a range of instruments to successfully handle challenging emotions.

Building Self-Regulation Skills

Self-regulation is the capacity to control, in a healthy manner, your feelings, ideas, and actions. Relationships are built and maintained in part by strong self-control abilities. How Important Is Self-Regulation? Self-regulation enables you to: React carefully rather than snapping to your feet. Get your demands across clearly. Set reasonable limits (Chapter 5 covers this). Constructively handle disagreement (discussed in

Chapter 6). Building Blocks of Self-Regulation:
Determine Your Triggers: Figure out what circumstances or actions usually make you feel strongly (Chapter 3 covers this). Exercise mindfulness to become more conscious of your feelings before they worsen and result in negative actions. Take Breaks: Give yourself some time to collect yourself if you're feeling overburdened, then get back into the action. Relaxation Techniques: As was already indicated, relaxation techniques can be quite effective instruments for self-control.

Chapter 8: Mindfulness and Stress Management

Developing Peace and Happiness in Partnerships Although they can bring about a lot of happiness and connection, relationships can also cause stress. Conflicts, miscommunications, and outside influences can be detrimental to our mental health. This chapter examines how practicing mindfulness and stress reduction might help you develop inner peace and deal with relationship difficulties more resiliently.

Emotional Awareness via Mindfulness Practices

The practice of mindfulness involves focusing attention on the current moment without passing judgment. It entails developing an objective, detached awareness of your ideas, feelings, and physical experiences. Developing mindfulness is a great way to become more emotionally aware in relationships.

Relationship Benefits of Mindfulness:

Enhanced communication: You can express your emotions more efficiently and clearly if you are more conscious of them (as discussed in Chapter 5).

Enhanced empathy: As we discuss in Chapter 4, mindfulness enables you to comprehend other people's emotional experiences on a deeper level.

Decreased reactivity: You can pick your reactions to stressful events rather than immediately reacting by analyzing your feelings without passing judgment. Techniques for Mindfulness: Focusing your attention and calming your mind are the two main goals of meditation. There are numerous approaches to meditation; some concentrate on the breath, physical experiences, or mantras.

Mindful Movement: Exercises that mix mindfulness and physical movement, such as yoga or tai chi, are beneficial for mental and physical health.

Breathing mindfully: Taking deep, calm breaths might help you manage challenging emotions in the moment by triggering your body's relaxation response. Mindful Observation: Throughout the day, stop sometimes to examine your environment, ideas, and emotions objectively.

Methods for Stress and Anxiety Reduction

Anxiety and stress can be detrimental to our relationships. Being patient, empathetic, and having good communication skills are all more difficult when we're feeling overloaded. This subsection delves into methods for handling tension and worry, promoting more serene and satisfying relationships. Finding Stressors: Recognizing the circumstances or triggers in your relationships that contribute to stress is the first step towards controlling it. Exist any particular people, communication styles, or circumstances that make you feel more stressed? Good Coping Strategies: Create wholesome coping mechanisms for stress, such as: Frequent Exercise: Research has shown that exercise is an effective way to reduce stress. Discover your passions, be they team sports, dance, or strolling. Methods of Relaxation: Techniques to help relax and lower stress include progressive muscle relaxation, guided imagery, and deep breathing. Time management: To prevent feeling overburdened by obligations, learn efficient time management techniques. Establishing Boundaries (Chapter 5): Significantly lowering stress can be achieved by learning to say no and placing your health first. Creating a Support System: Having a solid network of friends, family, or a therapist at your side can offer priceless emotional support and teach you healthy coping mechanisms for stressful situations.

Value of Unwinding and Taking Care of Oneself

Maintaining your physical and emotional well-being is crucial for exhibiting your full potential in relationships, therefore self-care is not selfish. The advantages of self-care decreased worry and tension increased vitality and happiness Enhanced adaptability and capacity to handle difficulties increased capacity for compassion and empathy Self-Healing Techniques: Sleeping Enough: Try to get between seven and eight hours of good sleep every night. Healthy Eating: Fuel your body

with wholesome foods that provide you with long-lasting energy.
Taking Part in Activities You Enjoy: Schedule time for interests and pastimes that relax and make you happy.
Spending Time in Nature: Being in nature can be a very effective way to reduce stress and improve your mood.
Creating Bonds with Loved Ones: Social connections and a sense of community are enhanced when you spend time with encouraging individuals. Recall that practicing mindfulness, controlling stress, and placing self-care first are lifelong habits.

Celebrate your accomplishments, have patience with yourself, and don't be afraid to get professional assistance if you need it. The next chapter will address the significance of creating and preserving a strong support network, which is an essential component of cultivating happy, healthy relationships all the way through life.

Chapter 9: Building a Healthy Foundation: Mind, Body, and Relationships

This chapter examines the relationship between physical and mental health. It explores the ways in which maintaining your physical health can improve your mental condition and vice versa. It also highlights how crucial it is to get professional assistance when necessary in order to overcome emotional obstacles and forge greater bonds with others.

Restorative Sleep Practices for Emotional Balance

A vital human requirement, sleep is essential to one's physical and emotional well-being. Lack of good sleep increases the likelihood of experiencing: Movability and erratic behavior difficulty focusing and concentrating Anxiety and stress levels rising inability to control one's emotions Making Sleep a Priority to Improve Emotional Health:
Establish a Regular Sleep Schedule: Even on weekends, go to bed and wake up at roughly the same

time every day. This aids in maintaining the normal sleep-wake cycle of your body.
Establish a Calm Bedtime Schedule: Before going to bed, unwind with peaceful pursuits like music listening, warm baths, or reading. Spend at least one hour before bedtime avoiding stimulating activities, such as screen time. Enhance Your Sleep Environment To encourage sound sleep, make sure your bedroom is cool, quiet, dark, and clutter-free.
Frequent Workout: Exercise can help you sleep better, but avoid doing intense exercises right before bed. Limit alcohol and caffeine as these chemicals can interfere with sleep cycles. Cut back on your consumption, particularly in the afternoon and at night.

The Benefits of Physical Activity for Mental Health

Frequent exercise is a great way to support mental well-being in addition to its positive effects on physical health. Exercise can improve your mental health in the following ways:
Lessens Stress and Anxiety: Exercise releases endorphins, which are feel-good hormones that can also aid in stress management.
Enhances Sleep Quality: Frequent exercise can encourage more restful, deeper sleep, which boosts energy and enhances emotional control.
Enhances Self-Esteem: Reaching fitness objectives and experiencing physical strength can help build confidence

and a good self-image. Lessens Depressive Symptoms:
Research has demonstrated that exercise is a useful
tool for treating mild to moderate depressive symptoms.
Choosing Pleasurable Activities: Choosing activities you
enjoy and can do over time is the key to gaining the
mental health advantages of exercise.
Examine several choices, such as: Team activities
Strolling or sprinting Dance Yoga, Cycling, Swimming,

Obtaining Expert Assistance When Necessary

When life presents difficulties that appear
insurmountable, it's acceptable to seek expert
assistance. Trained mental health specialists, therapists
and counselors can offer support, direction, and
evidence-based techniques for handling emotional
challenges.
When to Think About Getting Professional Assistance:
feeling depressed, anxious, or stressed out for long
lengths of time inability to handle relationships or daily
responsibilities Taking part in harmful or unhealthy
activities Noticing notable variations in sleep or appetite
Considering suicide or self-harm Selecting the
Appropriate Therapist: There are numerous techniques
to therapy, therefore it's critical to choose a therapist
with whom you click. Until you locate a therapist that fits
your needs and tastes, don't be afraid to ask questions
and conduct interviews with potential candidates.
Remind yourself that maintaining your physical and

emotional well-being are equally crucial. By making regular exercise, getting enough sleep, and getting help when you need it a priority, you're laying a solid foundation for overcoming obstacles in life and cultivating happy, healthy relationships.

Chapter 10: Cultivating Thriving Relationships: Building Trust, Appreciation, and Communication

A satisfying existence is based on having relationships. They provide us affection, encouragement, and a feeling of community. However, it takes constant work and dedication to keep relationships in good shape. This chapter examines the essential components that go into creating solid, long-lasting bonds.

Establishing Mutual Respect and Trust

Healthy relationships are built on the foundations of respect and trust. Because you know that people you trust will treat your feelings and information with respect, you may be open and honest with them. Respect recognizes the intrinsic worth of the other individual as well as their viewpoints.

Establishing Trust: Integrity and Honesty: Act and speak with sincerity. Acknowledge responsibility for errors made and endeavor to restore confidence.

Reliability: Honor your word and show that you are a trustworthy person.

Confidentiality: Maintain shared confidences and show consideration for others' privacy.
Acting with Respect: Active Listening (discussed in Chapter 4): Pay great attention to what the other person is saying, both with words and body language.
Empathy: Seek to comprehend the thoughts and emotions of the other person (discussed in Chapter 4).
Validation: Even if you disagree with the other person's ideas or feelings, acknowledge them anyway.
Positive Regard: Treat the other person with dignity and gratitude for their uniqueness.

Relationship Communication That Works

Building and sustaining successful relationships requires clear and constant communication. It enables you to communicate your needs and emotions, comprehend other people, and resolve conflicts amicably (discussed in Chapters 5 and 6). The Significance of "I" Statements: As discussed in Chapter 5, utilize "I" statements to assertively and blamelessly communicate your demands and feelings. For instance: "I feel hurt when plans change at the last minute because I value quality time together." Engage in Active Listening by observing the speaker's nonverbal and vocal signals. To be sure you understand, make sure you ask clarifying questions and sum up what you've heard.

Healthy Debate vs. Destructive Arguments: Although disagreements are unavoidable, they can present chances for development if handled civilly. Don't interrupt, call names, or make personal assaults.
Instead of placing blame, concentrate on coming up with solutions (discussed in Chapter 6).
Nonverbal Communication: Expressions on your face, tone of voice, and body language all help convey messages. Make sure your spoken message and your nonverbal clues are consistent.

Putting Gratitude and Appreciation Into Practice

By expressing your thankfulness and appreciation for the good things in your relationships, you may make them stronger and promote each other's wellbeing. The Power of Appreciation: You may make a big difference in your relationships by taking the time to recognize their positive aspects. It communicates to the other person your appreciation for their contributions.
Easy Ways to Express Thank You: Thank you verbally. Compose a heartfelt card or note. Make a nice gesture by running errands or offering assistance with a duty. Take time to appreciate activities that you both enjoy doing together. The Advantages of Appreciation Gratitude is a powerful tool that can improve your relationships and general well-being. It can increase resilience, lessen stress, and increase enjoyment.
Sustaining Good Relationships: A Continuous Process

Developing and maintaining good connections takes time and effort. Along the route, there will be ups and downs. You can build solid and encouraging relationships that improve your life by placing a high value on appreciation, good communication, trust, and respect for others.

Recall: Relationships that are healthy require reciprocity. Time and effort must be put in by both partners. Sustaining wholesome relationships requires forgiveness, which is discussed in Chapter 6. Setting limits and placing your health first is acceptable (discussed in Chapter 5). If you're having relationship problems, you might want to contact a therapist or counselor for assistance. Other relationship-related topics including handling conflict, controlling strong emotions, and establishing appropriate boundaries will be covered in the upcoming chapters.

Chapter 11: The Path to Healing: Forgiveness, Self-Love, and Moving Forward

Experiences, both good and bad, abound in life. We occasionally come across circumstances that make us feel wounded, enraged, or deceived. Retaining these bad feelings can be a weight, making it more difficult for us to go on and have happy relationships. With the help of this chapter's exploration of the ideas of emotional healing, self-love, and forgiveness, you will be better equipped to create a happier and more satisfying life.

Releasing Resentment and Fury

Anger and resentment are normal reactions to being injured. But holding on to these feelings might be like having a big burden. To forgive is to free yourself from the weight of negativity, not to approve of the deeds of others.

The Consequences of Unresolved Anger: Persistent anger can have detrimental effects on your relationships, job, general well-being, and physical and mental health.

Comprehending Forgiveness: It requires time and effort and is an individual process. It doesn't imply moving on from the incident or making amends with the person who wronged you. Letting go of the negativity and making the decision to go forward with a lighter heart is what forgiveness is all about
. Advantages of Pardoning:
Pardoning can: Diminish tension and unease enhance your physical well-being Encourage more wholesome partnerships Let go of the past and move forward.
Letting Go Techniques: Journaling: Expressing and processing your emotions through written word can be beneficial.
Positive Self-Talk: Dispell unfavorable ideas you may have about the circumstances or yourself.
Concentrate on the Present: You can loosen your hold on the past and firmly establish yourself in the here and now by engaging in mindfulness exercises. Empathy (for oneself): Make an effort to comprehend the reasons behind your possible anger or rage.

Progressing Towards Emotional Recovery

Recovering from emotional trauma is a process rather than a final goal. Even if there will be obstacles on your path, you can get closer to a state of higher emotional well-being by engaging in self-compassionate behavior and using constructive coping techniques.

Self-compassion: Treat yourself with kindness and compassion. Give yourself permission to feel your feelings and acknowledge your grief.
Healthy Coping Mechanisms: Take part in hobbies, physical activity, and outdoor pursuits that enhance emotional stability and relaxation. (discussed in Chapter 8)
Creating a Support System: Be in the company of caring, upbeat people who are supportive of you. (explained in Chapter 9)
 Getting Professional Assistance: You might want to think about seeing a therapist or counselor if you're having trouble managing on your own.

Acceptance and Love of Oneself

A positive relationship with yourself is built on self-love. It entails treating oneself with care and respect and embracing who you are, flaws and all.
The Significance of Self-Love: Having self-love and acceptance makes it easier for you to form wholesome bonds with other people. Additionally, it promotes resiliency in the face of difficulties. Growing in Self-Love Determine Your Strengths: Pay attention to your advantages and successes.
Engage in Self-Care: Schedule time for mental, physical, and spiritual stimulation. (discussed in Chapters 8 and 9)
Establish Positive Objectives: Take on healthy challenges for yourself and acknowledge your accomplishments.

Difficulty Negative Self-Talk: Swap out your self-defeating ideas with more realistic and upbeat ones. Recall that emotional healing, self-love, and forgiveness are all continual processes.

Celebrate your accomplishments and have patience with yourself. Your journey towards creating a happier and more satisfying life will begin when you make the decision to let go of negativity and accept self-compassion. The importance of social skills and communication in managing the intricacies of social interactions will be discussed in the last chapter.

Chapter 12: Cultivating Your Circle: Building a Positive Support System

A network of people who show you love, support, and acceptance is a powerful support system. They are the people you can count on to lend you a sympathetic ear, a sympathetic shoulder, or a helpful hand. This chapter looks at the value of creating a network of supportive people and how to keep these important relationships going.

Recognizing Good Relationships

Relationships are not all made equal. The people in your healthy support network are those who appreciate, encourage, and elevate you. The following are some traits of wholesome relationships:

Respect and Trust: With these people, you feel free to be who you are and feel safe. They respect your viewpoints and opinions. (explained in Chapter 10)

Open Communication: You are free to share your ideas and emotions without fear of repercussions. They pay attention to you and are attentive listeners. (discussed in Chapter 5)

Positive Influence: They encourage you to reach your full potential and stand by your aspirations.

Mutual Assistance: Collaboration is a two-way street. You are also available to them, providing assistance and motivation.

Embracing a Positive Environment

The individuals you spend time with have a big influence on your general wellbeing. You may cultivate an atmosphere that promotes resilience, growth, and happiness by surrounding oneself with good and encouraging people.

Recognize Bad Relationships: Consider your feelings following interactions with particular individuals. Do they sap your vitality or cause you to feel self-conscious? It may be time to put negativity behind you.

Increasing the Size of Your Social Network: Engage in hobbies and pursuits that will introduce you to new people that are passionate about and share your ideals.

Taking Care of Current Relationships: Schedule time for the people who are important to you and are already a part of your life. Express your concern for them with your words and deeds.

Techniques for Forming Powerful Bonds:

Be a Good Listener: Take the time to actively hear what people have to say and demonstrate a sincere interest in them.

Provide Support: Show your loved ones that you are there for them when they need you. Provide supportive words, a sympathetic ear, or useful assistance.

Be Reliable: Honor your word and establish yourself as a trustworthy individual. Be Positive: Keep an upbeat attitude and concentrate on life's positive aspects. Don't strive to be someone you're not; just be yourself. For real connections to be made, authenticity is essential.

The Value of Returning the Favor

Not only does helping others benefit the one receiving it, but it can also bolster your own sense of wellbeing and support network. Giving back can have a positive impact on a social network in the following ways:

Increasing Your Circle: You can meet new people who are motivated to change the world by volunteering or taking part in community events.

Strengthening Bonds: Having a team and working toward a common objective together can help people feel like they belong.

Developing Confidence: You might feel more confident and good about yourself when you help others and see the wonderful difference you can make.

Discovering Purpose: You can find meaning and purpose in your life by making a contribution to something greater than yourself. Recall that creating a network of supportive people is a continuous activity. It requires deliberateness, time, and effort. You may build a network of dependable individuals who improve your life and your general well-being by fostering current relationships, widening your social circle, and giving back to your community. Engaging in proactive assistance to others is an investment in strengthening your own social network in addition to giving back.

Conclusion: Recap: Key Takeaways and Continued Growth

This thorough manual covered a wide range of topics related to establishing and preserving wholesome relationships. Here's a rundown of the main conclusions: The cornerstone of a healthy relationship is efficient communication, emotional intelligence, and self-awareness. These qualities are essential for creating lasting bonds. Chapters 4, 5, and 7 explore this topic. The significance of constructive coping strategies To effectively negotiate problems in your relationships, learn appropriate coping mechanisms for stressful situations and tough emotions. Referred to in Chapters 8 The effectiveness of awareness Better relationships can be fostered by mindfulness techniques, which can increase emotional awareness, boost communication, and lower stress. (discussed in Chapter 8) The significance of respect and trust: Strong relationships are built on a foundation of respect and trust. They permit frank conversation, honesty, and vulnerability. (explained in Chapter 10) Proficiency in communication abilities: Being able to articulate your needs, comprehend others, and resolve conflicts in a positive way all depend on your ability to communicate clearly and assertively, which includes active listening. Referred to in Chapters 5 and 6 The influence of thankfulness and appreciation:

Thanking others for their positive contributions to your relationships improves the relationship and promotes wellbeing. (explained in Chapter 10) The value of pardoning Giving up bitterness and rage enables you to heal from emotional trauma and develop inner tranquility. (explained in Chapter 11) Self-love and acceptance: The cornerstone of wholesome relationships with oneself and other people is the development of self-compassion and self-acceptance. (explained in Chapter 11) The importance of having a supportive network: Your well-being can be greatly improved by surrounding oneself with positive and encouraging people. (explained in Chapter 12)

Sustained Expansion Creating and preserving wholesome relationships takes a lifetime to complete. Here are some ideas for continuing your growth: Engage in self-reflection: Consider your relationship dynamics, emotional reactions, and communication styles on a regular basis.

Look for opportunities to learn: Learn about relationship dynamics, emotional intelligence, and communication by reading books, articles, or watching videos. Join a group for support: Making connections with people who are attempting to create wholesome relationships can be energizing and insightful. Think about expert advice: Support and guidance might be provided by a therapist or counselor if you are facing particular relationship difficulties. Recall to be gentle with yourself. It takes time and work to grow. Enjoy the process of developing deeper, more satisfying connections throughout your life and celebrate your accomplishments.You may build enduring, satisfying relationships that improve both your life and the lives of people around you by continuing to study, develop, and put the skills described in this guide into practice.

© Lucky Willis

www.ingramcontent.com/pod-product-compliance
Lightning Source LLC
Chambersburg PA
CBHW051850250726
48659CB00006B/2132